1920
Swimsuit worn
in Honolulu
during return
from Australia

Tom Tierney

Edward, Prince of Wales

1911
At his investiture as Prince of Wales,
Caernarvon Castle

PLATE 1

1920
Dressed for the country

At the races

PLATE 2

1921
Dressed as a Bengal Lancer
during his Indian tour

1922
On a visit to Japan

PLATE 3

As Royal Commander of the Guards   In Royal Navy ceremonial uniform

PLATE 4

3

1934
Bathing costume
worn on a trip
to Biarritz
with Edward

Tom Tierney

Wallis Warfield
Spencer Simpson

1934
Court presentation gown

PLATE 5

1937
In the garden of the Château de Candé,
awaiting the arrival of Edward

In the gown copied by
Madame Tussaud's waxworks to dress
their effigy of the Duchess

PLATE 6

1936
Clothes worn on the island of Rab
during a Dalmatian coast cruise
aboard the yacht *Nahlin*

PLATE 7

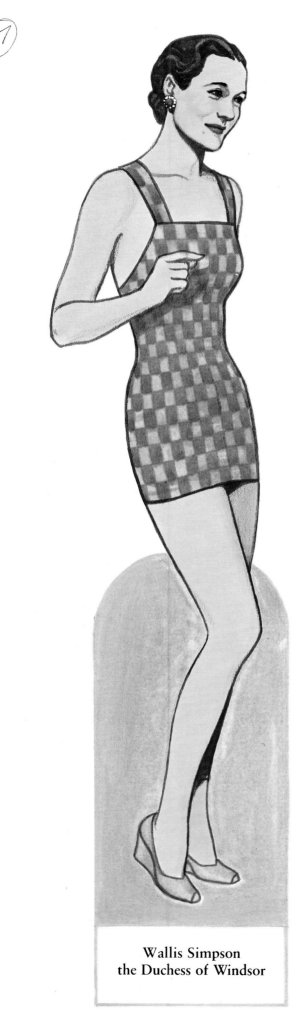

**Wallis Simpson
the Duchess of Windsor**

**King Edward VIII
later the Duke of Windsor**

1936
Bathing costumes worn during the cruise aboard the *Nahlin*

PLATE 8

Wedding costumes, June 3, 1937

Do not cut out white
area between arm
and body.

Crepe satin gown of specially dyed
"Wallis" blue, by Mainbocher;
hat, of straw, feathers and tulle, by Reboux;
sapphire and diamond bracelet by Van Cleef

Formal day wear of cutaway coat,
double-breasted vest and striped trousers

PLATE 9

1937
Costumes worn in Venice during the honeymoon

PLATE 10

1937
Costumes worn at Schloss Wasserleonburg, Austria,
during the honeymoon

PLATE 11

Do not cut out white area
between arm and body.

1937
Silver lamé gown by Mainbocher;
sapphire and diamond jewelry

1940
Chanel gown worn during last days in Paris
before the German occupation

PLATE 12

French Red Cross uniform
at the beginning of World War II

As major general with
the British military mission in France

PLATE 13

Do not cut out white area
between arm and body.

1950s
Dior New Look gown with silver brocade;
at a New York party

PLATE 14

Do not cut out white area
between arm and body.

1950s
Ball gown

1950
Masked ball costume

PLATE 15